Usborne Spotter's Guides

HOR
& POI

D0284882

Joanna Spector
Illustrated by David Wright, Elaine Keenan
and Malcolm McGregor

Edited by Alastair Smith, Felicity Mansfield and Tim Dowley
Designed by Karen Tomlins and Joanne Kirkby
Series designer: Laura Fearn
Cover designer: Joanne Kirkby
Additional illustrations: Andy Martin and Ed Roberts
Expert consultant: Juliet Mander

Acknowledgements:
Cover © Mark J. Barrett/Alamy;
1, 2–3, 10–11 © Kit Houghton Photography/Corbis;
4–5 – © W. Perry Conway/Corbis; 6–7 © Peter Johnson/Corbis;
7(mr) Digital Vision; 12–13 © Annie Griffiths Belt/Corbis;
14–15, 18, 19 © Kit Houghton Photography;
16–17 © Buddy Mays/Corbis

This edition first published in 2006 by Usborne Publishing Ltd.,
Usborne House, 83–85 Saffron Hill, London, EC1N 8RT, England.
www.usborne.com

Copyright © 2006, 2001, 1979 Usborne Publishing Ltd.
The name Usborne and the devices are Trade Marks
of Usborne Publishing Ltd.

All rights reserved. No part of this publication may
be reproduced, stored in a retrieval system or
transmitted in any form or by any means,
electronic, mechanical, photocopying,
recording, or otherwise, without the
prior permission of the publisher.

Printed in China

CONTENTS

4 How to use this book
6 The story of horses
7 Using horses
8 Looking at horses
9 Colours and markings
10 Points of the horse
12 Horse and pony care
13 Stabling
14 Feeding
16 Grooming
17 Shoeing
18 Riding
19 Tack
20 Ponies
32 Riding horses
46 Harness horses
53 Draught horses
60 Internet links
61 Useful words
62 Spotter's chart
64 Index

HOW TO USE THIS BOOK

This book is a guide to identifying horse and pony breeds from all over the world. The breeds are arranged with ponies first, followed by riding horses, harness horses (bred to pull light carriages) and draught horses (used for pulling heavy loads).

Next to each picture is a short description of the breed, telling you where it originated, what kind of work it was bred for, the colours it can be, and its height.

Some colours and markings have unusual names. You can look them up on page 9. If there are any other words you don't understand, look in the list of useful words on page 61, or check the diagram detailing horse parts on pages 10-11.

These horses live wild on the Great Plains in Wyoming, USA. They are descended from riding horses.

Throughout this book, you will find suggested links to horse and pony websites. For a complete list of links and instructions, turn to page 60.

SPOTTING A BREED

When you see a breed, make a tick in the circle next to its description. Some types of horse live only in certain parts of the world, and others are very rare indeed. However, you might spot them in wildlife parks, in movies or on the television.

The chart on pages 62-63 lists every breed shown in this book. Note the date that you see each breed on the chart. You'll build up a record of the breeds that you've spotted.

Name of breed	Date
Dartmoor	*08/06/06*
Døle	*08/06/06*
Don	*05/07/07*
Dutch Draught	*10/11/06*

Fill in the chart like this.

THE STORY OF HORSES

The first horses were small and deer-like. They lived in woodlands, 50 million years ago. They evolved into swift, sure-footed beasts that were good at escaping from enemies.

All modern breeds of horse are descended from two ancient types, the southern type and the northern type.

Humans are thought to have begun to control and breed horses in Europe, several thousand years ago. Today, there are about 200 different breeds of horses.

The only truly wild breed left in the world is the Przewalski, from the Gobi Desert in Mongolia, where some still live in herds.

The southern type was light and swift, with a silky coat, like a modern Arab horse.

These horses' long legs and slender bodies are signs that they are descended from southern-type horses.

The northern type had a thick, rough coat and sturdy legs, like a modern Exmoor pony.

For a link to online exhibits from a horse museum, turn to page 60.

USING HORSES

Originally, horses were hunted for food. Later, they were bred for specific types of work. For example, some were bred to pull light carts and carriages day after day. Heavier types, meanwhile, were bred for ploughing and pulling heavy carts and wagons.

Today, people ride mostly for pleasure or sport, although some horses still work on farms, especially in poorer countries.

In the 1800s Arab horses, which are small, nimble and swift, were crossed with English hunters, which are strong and hardy, to produce Thoroughbreds. This fast, tall and beautiful breed is now used for racing all over the world.

Racing Thoroughbreds

LOOKING AT HORSES

At first, it can be tricky to tell what breed a horse or pony is. Here is a quick guide to certain clues.

A curved-in face (called a dished profile) and a tail held high means that the animal probably has some Arab blood.

A small, sturdy build and a long, rough coat are signs that it is probably a mountain or moorland pony.

A very tall, lightly built horse, with long legs, a fine skin and coat is probably a Thoroughbred.

A big, slow horse with heavy features and feather (long hairs) around its feet is probably a draught horse.

CROSS OR PURE BRED?

Most horses and ponies are cross-bred, that is, descended from different types. You are likely to see pure-bred horses and ponies at:

- Horse shows.
- Stud farms, where horses are bred.
- The breed's natural surroundings; for example, hills and moors in Britain, lowlands in France or Belgium, or mountains in Austria.
- Racing stables or racecourses.
- Riding stables.

COLOURS AND MARKINGS

Here are nine of the most common coat colours and patterns, and the proper names for them.

Bay

Chestnut

Black

Grey

Dun

Brown

Strawberry roan

Piebald

Skewbald

FACE MARKINGS

Star

Snip

Stripe

Blaze

LEG MARKINGS

Sock

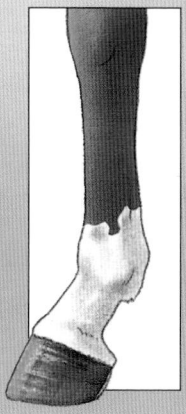

Stocking

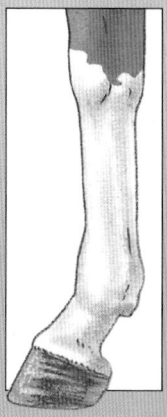

For links to websites with horse puzzles and quizzes, turn to page 60.

POINTS OF THE HORSE

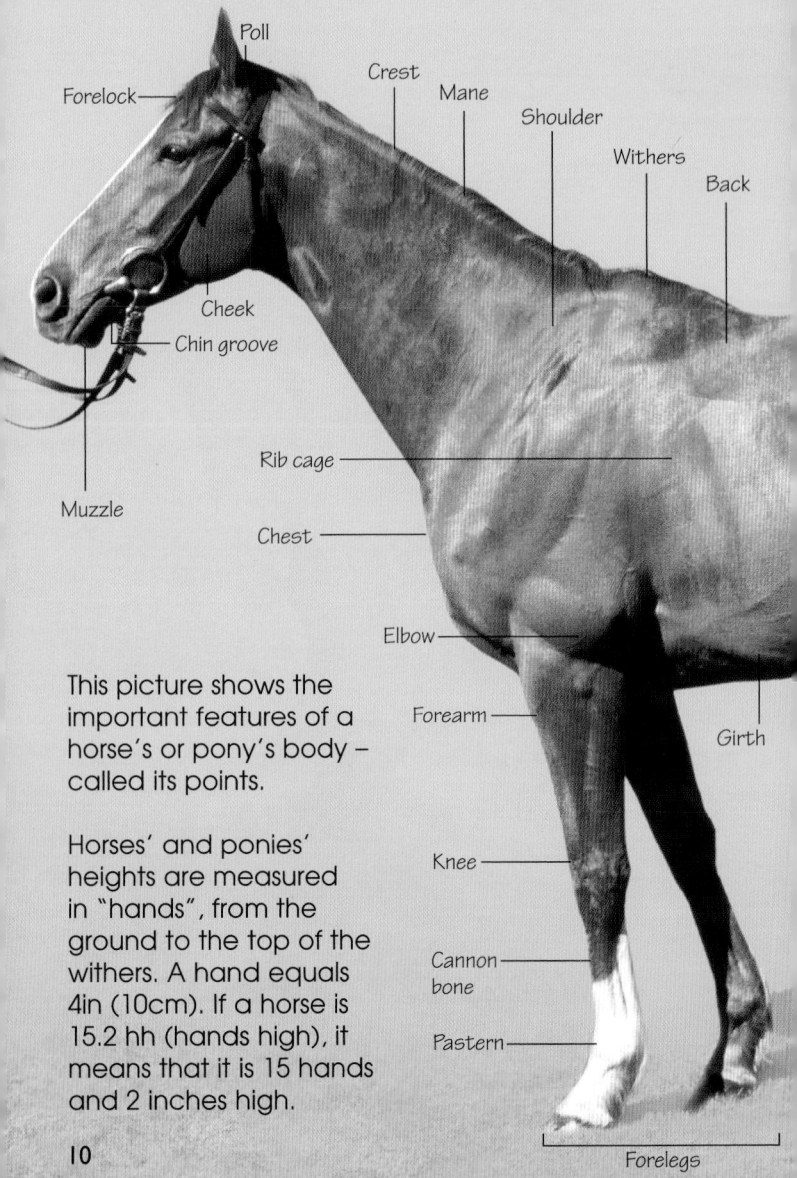

This picture shows the important features of a horse's or pony's body – called its points.

Horses' and ponies' heights are measured in "hands", from the ground to the top of the withers. A hand equals 4in (10cm). If a horse is 15.2 hh (hands high), it means that it is 15 hands and 2 inches high.

For a link to a quiz about the parts of a horse's body, turn to page 60.

HORSE OR PONY?

Whether an animal is called a horse or a pony depends on how tall it is. If it is over 14.2 hands high (hh) then it is classed as a horse. If it is 14.2hh, or less, then it is called a pony.

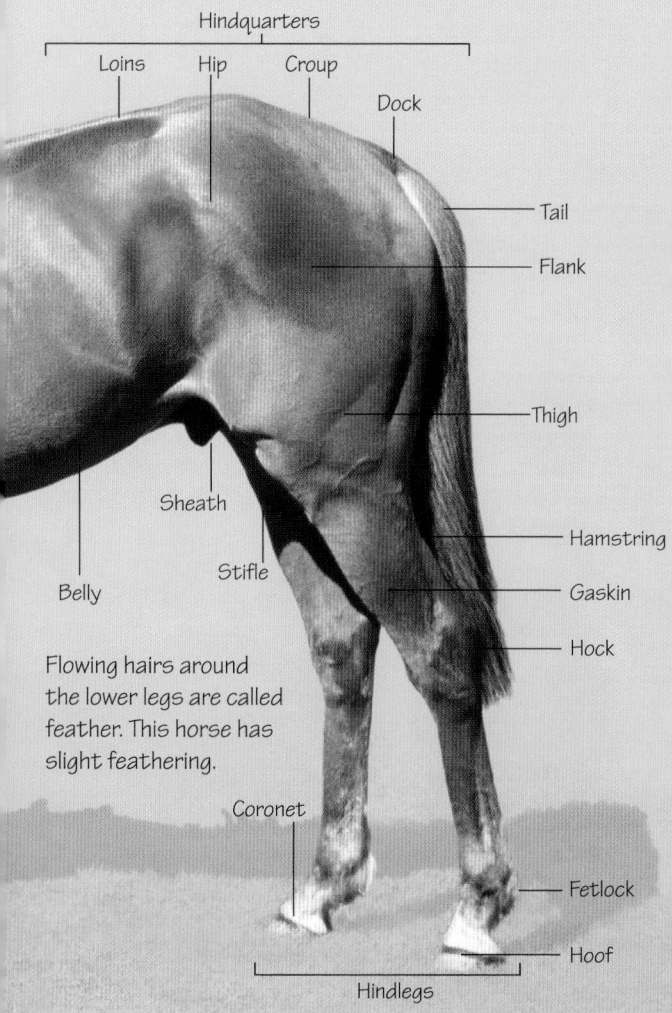

Flowing hairs around the lower legs are called feather. This horse has slight feathering.

HORSE AND PONY CARE

Wild horses and ponies live in groups, moving about together. To keep your horse or pony happy, let it live outside, as it would in the wild, as much as you can. To keep it healthy, follow these guidelines.

- Let it live in a field with other horses and ponies.
- Allow enough room for grazing. A pony needs at least 4000m^2 (one acre) to provide it with fresh grass.
- Change fields in spring and autumn if the grass is thinning, to allow the grass to grow back.
- Clear up droppings.
- Provide plenty of fresh drinking water.
- Make sure that there is shelter in the field, such as trees, or a shed.
- Ensure that the field's fencing is strong, to stop escape attempts. Also, make sure that fencing is safe, to prevent injuries.

Ponies enjoy the freedom of outdoor life.

STABLING

During really cold winter spells, you should keep your animal in a stable. Follow these tips so that it stays happy and healthy.

- Exercise the animal every day. Ride for an hour, or turn it out into the field for a few hours.
- Feed it properly. It needs hay to nibble during the day and night, and high-energy food such as corn, in the morning, at night and perhaps at midday.
- Give plenty of fresh drinking water.
- Clean the stable daily. Remove wet bedding and droppings to stop smells and foot disease.
- Put down fresh bedding regularly.
- Groom the horse every day, to keep its coat and skin clean and healthy.
- If your animal is clipped, it will need to wear rugs in winter. Seek advice from an expert, so that you know just how much protection is needed.
- Always let fresh air into the stable to lessen the chances of your animal catching coughs and colds.
- If you want to change your feeding and exercising routines, alter them gradually. Horses and ponies don't like change. They need time to adjust to new ways.

FEEDING

In its natural environment, a horse or pony eats small amounts of bulk food (mostly grass) almost non-stop throughout the day. Those kept in stables eat hay instead of grass. During the summer, horses and ponies are kept outside, and probably need no food other than grass. However, during the winter, they need a supplement of hay.

EXTRA FEEDS

As well as hay or grass, a horse may need high-energy or "short" feeds. Use corn or cubes, mixed with another type of food. (Corn is either oats or barley. Cubes are also called nuts.) You should seek advice from an expert about what would suit your animal best, and on how to prepare the food. Different horses have different needs.

Foods you can add to corn or cubes are:

- Bran, but only in small amounts.
- Chaff. This is made of chopped hay.
- Sugar beet, soaked for 24 hours prior to feeding.
- Small amounts of linseed, for a shiny coat.

For a link to an interactive guide to pony care, turn to page 60.

FEEDING GUIDELINES

How much, and what, you give to your horse or pony will depend on its size, temperament, health, how much exercise it gets, the time of year, and how much good grass is available.

These are the basic rules for feeding:

- Always make sure that it has enough grass or hay to eat.
- Feed a little and often. It will not be able to digest large meals properly.
- Always have fresh drinking water available.
- Wait for at least an hour after feeding before you ride your horse or pony.
- Give feeds at the same time each day.
- If there's no grass, give juicy vegetables or fruits, such as carrots or apples.
- Make sure that you give the animal access to a salt block.

Horses should have access to fresh water, particularly at feeding time.

GROOMING

There are lots of grooming tools. Each has a different use. Here's a selection.

• A hoof pick is used for cleaning inside the hooves.

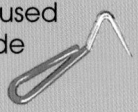

• Dirt and stains are taken off an unclipped coat with a dandy brush, working back from the top of the neck. Always brush in the direction of the coat.

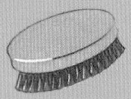

• If the animal is kept in a stable, a body brush can be used to clean the skin and coat. Don't use this brush on a field-kept horse, though – it strips the body oils that keep the animal warm, dry and healthy.

• A sweat scraper removes excess sweat or water from the coat.

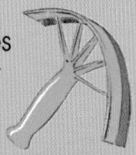

• A thin coat of hoof oil is brushed on the hooves to make them shine and stop them from splitting.

• Strapping pads are made of stuffed leather. Use them to groom the neck, shoulders and hind quarters, shortly after exercise. The pad shines the coat, and massages the muscles to tone them.

• A water brush is long and narrow, with short bristles. Used damp with water, for smoothing the mane and tail after brushing.

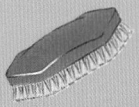

• Brushes are cleaned by pulling them across a rubber or metal currycomb.

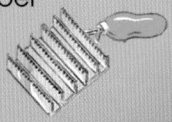

SHOEING

Most working horses and ponies need to wear metal shoes to stop their hooves from getting worn down. Shoes also stop the hoof becoming cracked, bruised or out of shape. Horseshoes must be made to fit properly, by a blacksmith – also called a farrier.

Unless a horse is being rested, new shoes should be fitted every 4-6 weeks. The shoes are nailed to the animal's hooves. It does not hurt, but some animals find the experience a little worrying at first.

PARTS OF THE HOOF

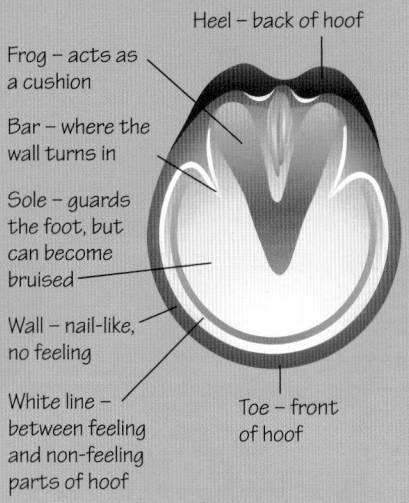

PARTS OF A SHOE

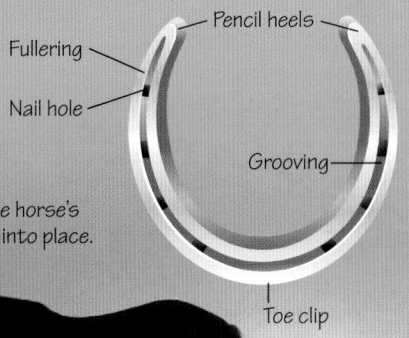

Shoes are shaped to fit the horse's feet before they are nailed into place.

RIDING

There are two main styles of riding:

- English style. This developed from an old European style of riding and is now practised all over the world.
- Western style. This grew out of cattle ranching work in North and South America. Mostly it is used in the Americas for rodeo displays, modern ranch work and long-distance trail riding.

Riders of either style learn to sit so that the horse is well balanced and can move freely. They learn to control a horse using a combination of their hands, legs, body and voice.

If you would like to learn to ride, find a riding school that is approved by a horse society, so you can be sure that your teacher is qualified.

English-style riding

For a link to a website with lots of horsey activities, turn to page 60.

TACK

ENGLISH SADDLE

Also called a "General Purpose Saddle".

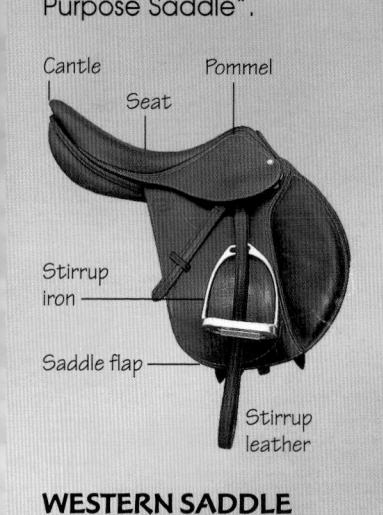

SNAFFLE BRIDLE

One of several bridles used in English-style riding.

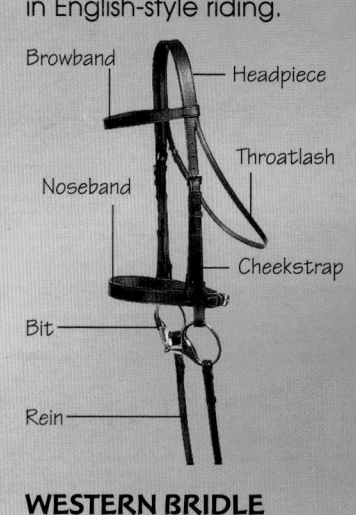

WESTERN SADDLE

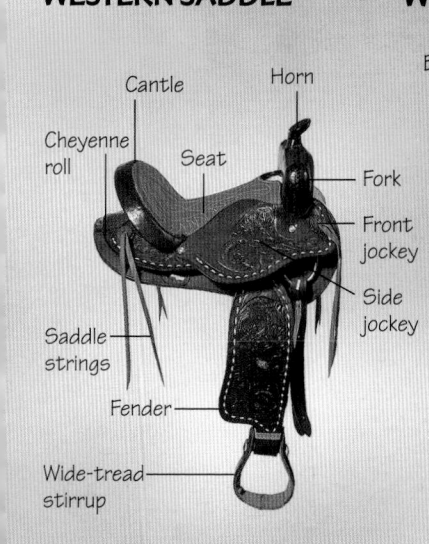

WESTERN BRIDLE

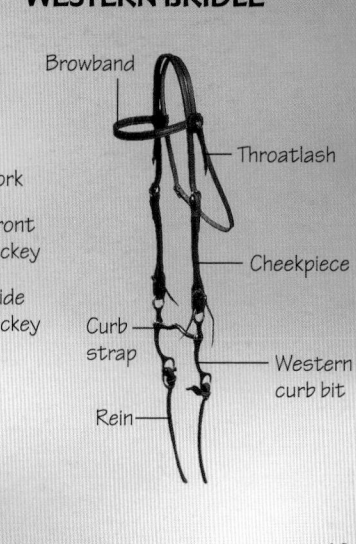

PONIES

⬇ HIGHLAND
Largest British pony. From the Scottish Highlands. Once used as a pack pony, now popular for trekking and driving. Usually grey or dun, can be black or chestnut. Up to 14.2hh.

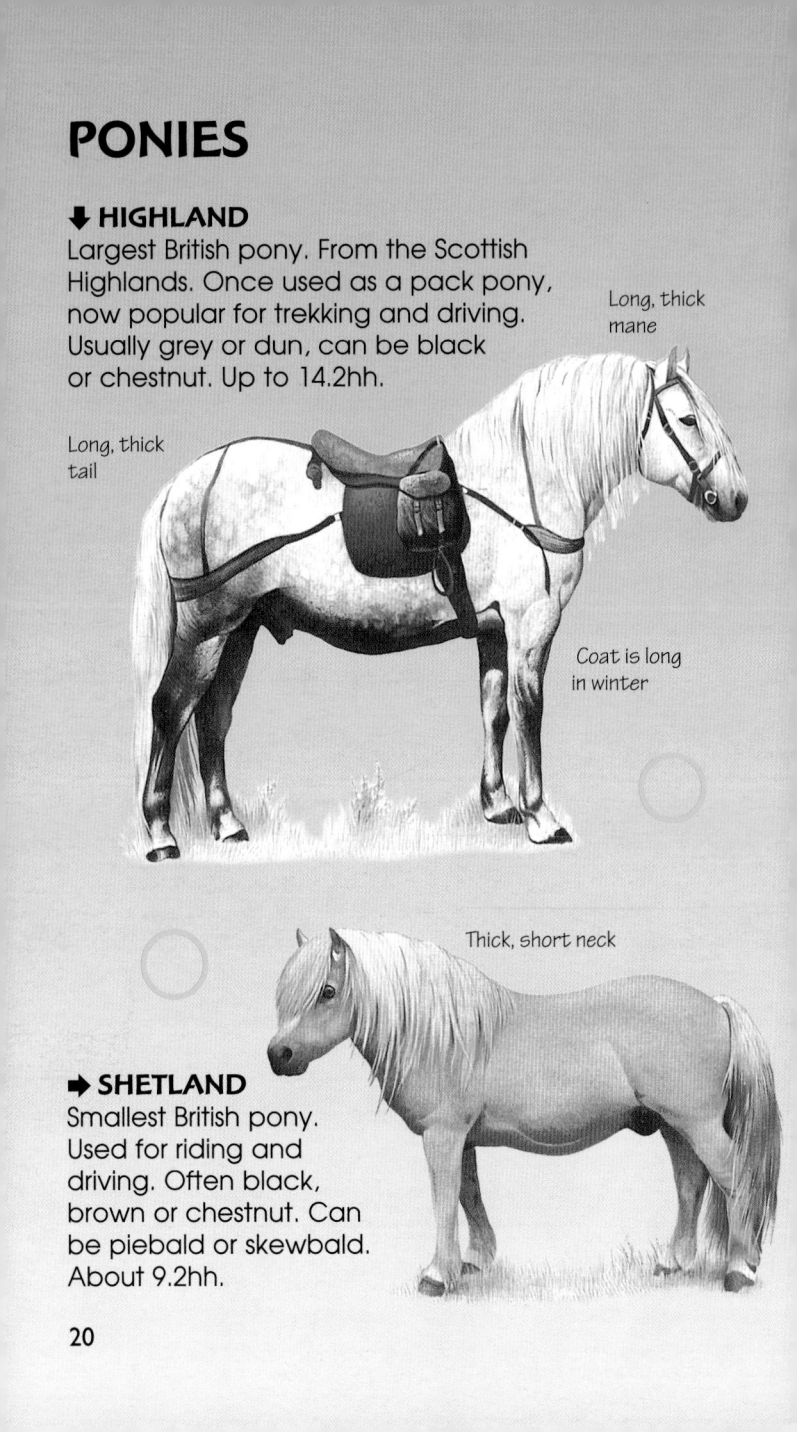

➡ SHETLAND
Smallest British pony. Used for riding and driving. Often black, brown or chestnut. Can be piebald or skewbald. About 9.2hh.

↓ DALE

From the Pennine hills, northern England. Used for pony trekking and as a harness pony. Usually dark brown or black. May have white markings. Up to 14.2hh.

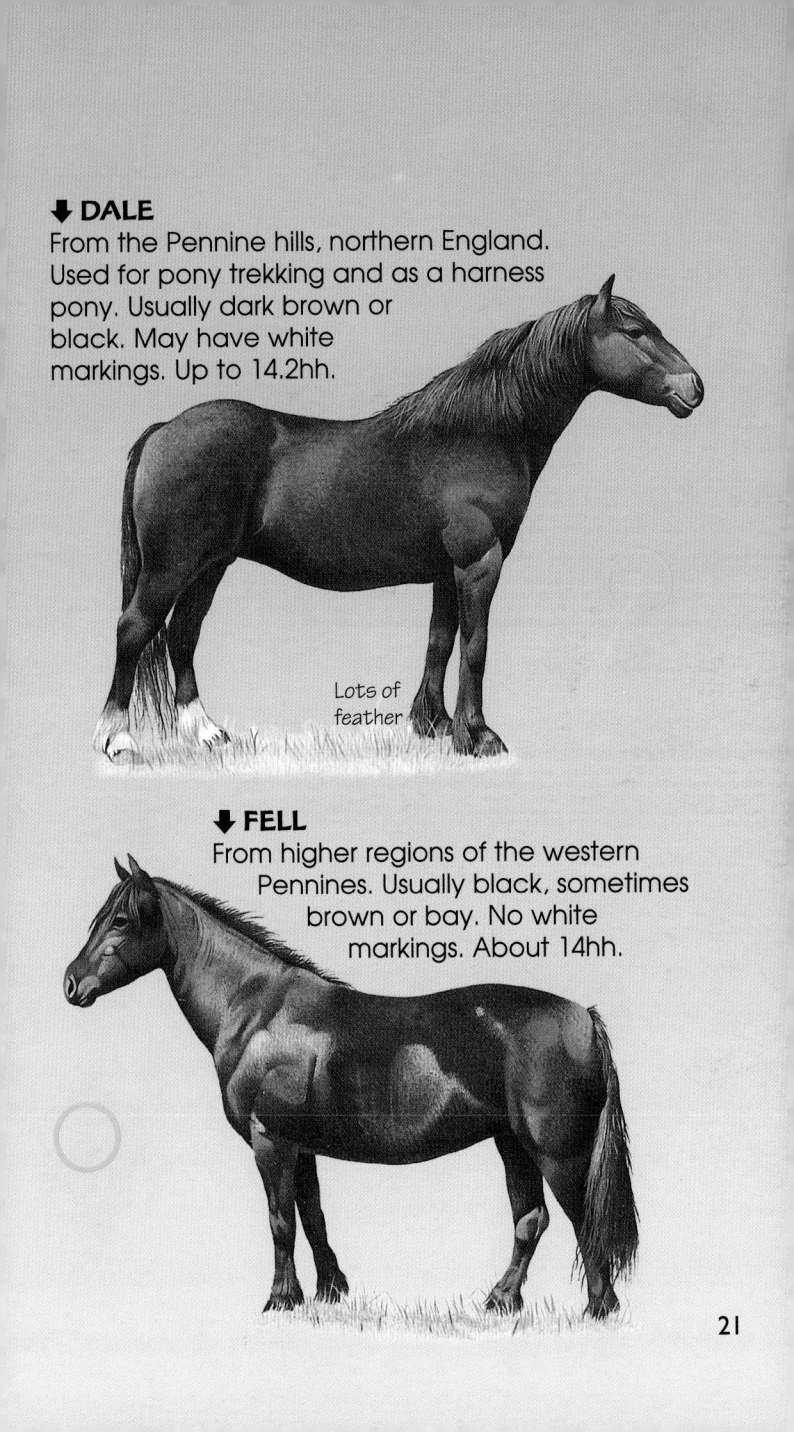

↓ FELL

From higher regions of the western Pennines. Usually black, sometimes brown or bay. No white markings. About 14hh.

PONIES

⬇ EXMOOR
Oldest British breed. Lives half wild on Exmoor, southwest England. Hardy. Good riding pony. Bay or brown with light-coloured underside. Up to 12.3hh.

⬇ DARTMOOR
Lives half wild on Dartmoor, southwest England. Hardy and sure-footed. Excellent riding pony. Bay, black or brown. About 12hh.

Small, pretty head

↓ CONNEMARA
From northwest Ireland. Ancestors probably Spanish and Arab horses. Jumps well. Usually grey, but often dun, black, brown, bay or chestnut. 13-14hh.

← NEW FOREST
From New Forest, southern England. Good riding pony. Size and markings vary, but not piebald or skewbald. Up to 14.2hh.

PONIES

↓ WELSH MOUNTAIN

Old breed from Wales which has Arab and Thoroughbred blood. Popular show pony. Great for children. Usually grey or chestnut. Up to 12hh.

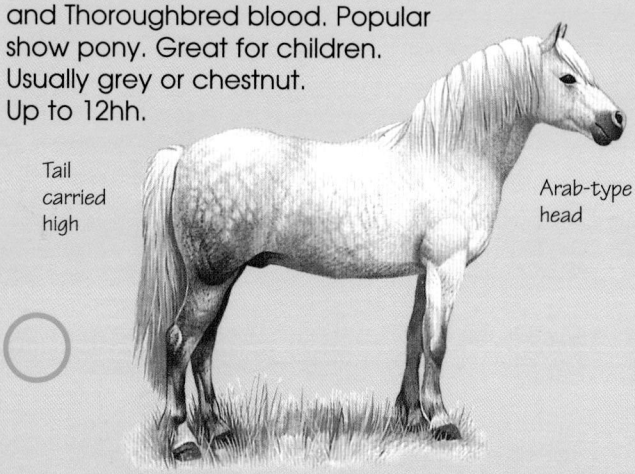

↓ WELSH COB

Descended from Welsh ponies and Andalusian horses. Strong. Most colours, except piebald or skewbald. 14-15hh.

⬇ HAFLINGER
From the Tyrol mountains, Austria. Strong and sure footed. Ideal for pulling heavy loads on steep hillsides. Good for riding and driving in harness. Chestnut. About 14hh.

➡ GOTLAND/RUSS
Originated on island of Gotland, Sweden, in Stone Age. Good trotter and jumper. All colours, often brown, bay or chestnut. About 13hh.

PONIES

↓ ICELANDIC
Bred from various northern European ponies. Used as riding or pack pony. Quiet and friendly. Any colour; often grey, dun, brown, black or chestnut.
12-13hh.

Lifts knees high when moving

Black and silver mane and tail. Mane grows short and straight, like a crest.

→ FJORD
Comes from Norway. Good for driving, haulage, carrying and riding. Mostly yellow-dun.
13-14hh.

➡ KAZAKH
From Russia. Used as a long-distance racing pony. Any colour; often bay, brown or chestnut. About 13hh.

⬇ HUÇUL
From the Carpathian mountains of Russia and Romania. Strong pack pony, probably related to Tarpan breed. Brown, dun or bay. About 13hh.

PONIES

⬇ CASPIAN
Wild pony, from Iran. Very few remaining. Looks like a miniature Thoroughbred. Good jumper. Usually bay or brown, sometimes grey. Never has white marking. 9.2-11.2hh.

➡ CRIOLLO
From South America. Survives well in poor conditions. Dun, roan, brown, skewbald, black, or bay. About 14.2hh.

⬇ CAMARGUE
From swampland at mouth of river Rhone, France. Tough and strong, many still live wild. Foals are born brown, but usually become grey. 14.2hh.

➡ FALABELLA
Miniature horse, from Argentina. Not strong, but used as a driving pony and children's pet. Any colour. Less than 7hh.

PONIES

↓ PRZEWALSKI
Also called Asiatic or Mongolian Wild Horse. Fewer than 1,500 exist – either in captivity or in herds on Gobi Desert, Mongolia. Bay or dun. 12-14hh.

↓ TARPAN
Oldest breed in Europe and northern Asia. Can be seen living wild in Poland. Usually brown with black ears, mane, tail and legs. 13hh.

Coarse mane and coat

For a link to a video clip of Przewalski horses, turn to page 60.

↓ PONY OF THE AMERICAS
New breed, from the USA. Good riding pony. Spotted. Looks similar to Appaloosa horse, though smaller. 11.2-13.2hh.

↓ SABLE ISLAND PONY
From Nova Scotia, Canada. Small and tough. Lives in wild herds. Feeds off scrub grass on sand dunes. Often chestnut.
About 14hh.

RIDING HORSES

⬇ THOROUGHBRED
Bred in England from Arab horses. World's fastest breed. Powerful and elegant. Black, brown, bay, grey or chestnut. 15-16.2hh.

➡ ANGLO-ARAB
Cross between Thoroughbred and Arab. Fast, strong, handsome. Excellent all-rounder. Same markings as Thoroughbred. About 16hh.

⬇ APPALOOSA
Bred by native North Americans. Good in all uses. Markings vary, though mainly identified by spots and splashes of pink and white. 14-15.3hh.

➡ AMERICAN SADDLEBRED
First bred as riding and harness horse in southern USA. An excellent riding horse. Bay, brown or chestnut. 15-15.3hh.

RIDING HORSES

↓ MORGAN
Originally bred from one American stallion named Justin Morgan. Solid, well-muscled. Bay, brown, black or chestnut.
14-15.2hh.

↓ TENNESSEE WALKING HORSE
From USA. Has three unusual gaits: flat-footed walk; running walk; running canter. Trots only when in harness. Solid markings.
15-16hh.

➡ QUARTER HORSE
From USA. Named after quarter-mile races. Quick and intelligent. Any colour. 15-16hh.

➡ PASO FINO
American, descended from Spanish explorers' horses. Does not trot at all. Can be any colour. 13-15.2hh.

RIDING HORSES

⬇ SHAGYA ARAB
Eastern European horse bred from Arabs. Tireless. Popular as cavalry horse in World War One. Usually grey. 14-15hh.

➡ POLISH ARAB
Bred in Poland since 1500. Used as general riding horse and racehorse. Tough and strong. Popular in USA and England. Can be bay, grey or chestnut. 14.2-15.1hh.

For a link to a website about the ways horses move, turn to page 60.

Straight profile

Thick, arched neck

➡ ANDALUSIAN
From southern Spain. Ancestors were Barb and Arab, plus native ponies. Good riding horse. Grey, black, bay or brown. 15.2-16hh.

⬇ LUSITANO
Portuguese horse. Same ancestry as Andalusian. Used by army, on farms and in bullrings. Grey, brown or bay. 15-16hh.

This horse is wearing special tack for the bullring.

RIDING HORSES

⬇ BUDYONNY
From Rostov, in Russia. Can live on poor food. Once used as a cavalry horse. Now often used for long-distance riding and racing. Brown, black, bay or chestnut. About 16hh.

⬅ DON
Comes from the Don Valley, Russia. Survives well on poor grass. Has lots of stamina. Always chestnut. 15-16hh.

High, narrow body

Fine coat with metallic sheen

➡ AKHAL-TEKE
Ancient breed from Turkmenistan. Has many uses. Can stand great heat or cold. Golden chestnut, bay, black or grey. About 15.1hh.

⬇ KARABAIR
Comes from the mountains of central Asia. Fast and good natured. Can work in dry, hot weather. Equally good for riding or in harness. Grey, bay, black or chestnut. 14.2-15.2hh.

Fine, thin tail

RIDING HORSES

↓ PALOMINO
Popular in the USA. Descended from Arab horses. The name can refer either to the breed or the colour. Bred mostly as show horses. Any shade of chestnut, with white mane and tail. 14-16hh.

← PINTO
Bred in the USA. There are two marking types: overo and tobiano. Overo is mostly dark, with white patches. Tobiano is mostly white, and has dark patches. Various heights.

➡ TURKOMAN
Comes from Turkmenistan and northern Iran. Strong and tireless. Good riding horse. Usually grey or bay; but also dun or chestnut. 14.3-15.2hh.

⬇ TRAKEHNER
Bred mainly in Poland and Germany. Used as a farm and cavalry horse. Gentle but brave. Very good sports horse. Bay, brown, black or chestnut. 16-16.2hh.

For a link to a website about a horse farm, turn to page 60.

RIDING HORSES

⬇ DØLE/GUDBRANDSAAL
Also called Ostland or Dølehest. From Norway. Strong, medium size. Originally used as a pack horse. Usually black, brown or bay. About 15hh.

➡ SELLE FRANCAIS
Cross-bred in France from Anglo-Arab and other horses. Brave and strong. Excellent for riding and sports, especially jumping. Often chestnut. 15.2-16.3hh.

⬇ HANOVERIAN
German breed descended from war horses ridden in the Middle Ages. Strong. Good sports horse. Any solid colour; often bay or brown. 16-17hh.

➡ HOLSTEIN
German breed. Big and strong. A good carriage and sports horse. Usually brown, bay or black. 16-16.2hh.

RIDING HORSES

➡ KNABSTRUP
Danish breed descended from a spotted Spanish mare. Popular as a circus horse. Fast and hardy. Always spotted, usually white with black spots. About 15hh.

Short, arched neck

⬅ LIPIZZANER
Used by the famous Spanish Riding School, Vienna, Austria. Bred from Andalusian horses. Excellent dressage horse; also good in harness. Born brown or black, changes to grey. Pure white in old age. 15-15.2hh.

For a link to a website with video clips of Lipizzaners, turn to page 60.

➡ BARB
From North Africa. Few pure-bred left. Can live on poor feed. Very fast over short distances. Bay, grey, black, brown or chestnut. 14-15hh.

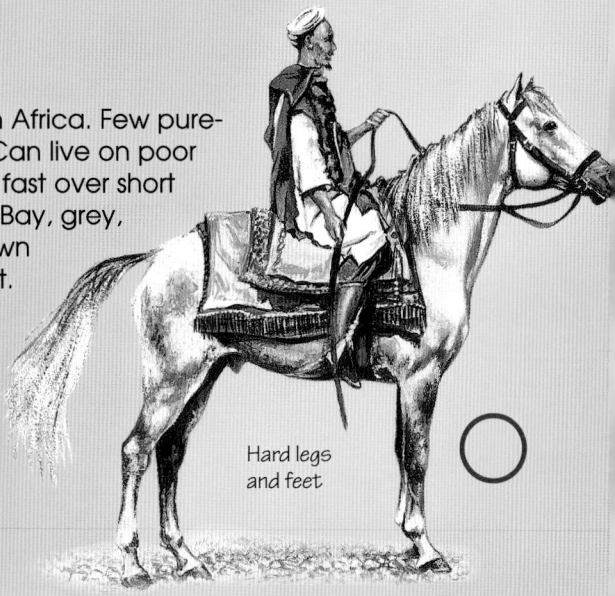

➡ WALER
First bred in New South Wales, Australia. Originally a cavalry horse. Now used for cattle herding, rodeos, show jumping and general riding. Any solid colour. 15-16hh.

HARNESS HORSES

➡ STANDARDBRED
Trotting horse, from the USA. The name comes from the fact that trotting horses had to achieve a certain speed, the "standard", before they were allowed to race. Any solid colour; usually bay, black or brown. 15-16hh.

➡ ORLOV TROTTER
From Russia, named after Count Orlov. Strong and fairly heavy. Once used as a cavalry horse. Often grey, also black or bay. 15.2-17hh.

➡ FRIESIAN
From Friesland, in the Netherlands. Bred in the Middle Ages to carry knights in armour. Strong and good natured. Always black. About 15hh.

⬇ GELDERLANDER
From Gelderland, in Netherlands. Once worked on farms. Now used for riding and harness work. Chestnut, grey, bay or brown. 15.2-16hh.

HARNESS HORSES

➡ GRONINGEN
Farm horse, from the Netherlands. Heavy, but fast. Can live on poor food. Good in harness or for riding. Usually black, bay or brown. 15.2-16hh.

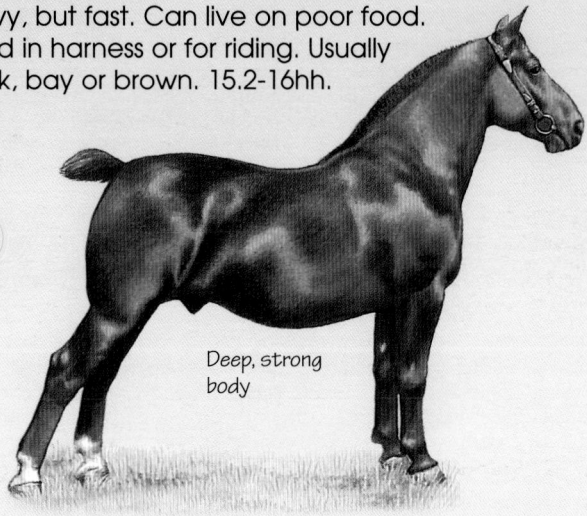

➡ OLDENBURGER
From northwest Germany. Big, strong, fairly fast. Popular carriage horse, used for riding, too. Usually grey, bay, black or brown. 16.2-17.2hh.

➡ CLEVELAND BAY
From Yorkshire, England. Sure footed, not fast. Used for carriage work. A good jumper. Always bay, without white markings. 16-16.2hh.

⬇ HACKNEY
English, high-stepping trotter, famous for exaggerated but graceful action. Popular at horse shows, it is often used to pull light carriages. Bay, black or brown. 14.3-15.3hh.

HARNESS HORSES

⬇ KUSTANAIR
From Kazakhstan, central Asia. Three types: Steppe, Riding and Basic. The Steppe is heavy and slow, Riding is light, and the Basic is between the two. Has solid colours, usually chestnut or bay. 15-15.2hh.

This is the lighter, "Basic" type of Kustanair.

➡ FINNISH
Used mainly on farms and in forests in Finland. Gentle and tireless. Also used for trotting races and riding. Most are chestnut, often with white markings. About 15.2hh.

➡ FREDERIKSBORG
An old breed from Denmark. Hard working. Used on farms and for riding. Strong and lively. Usually chestnut. Up to 16hh.

⬇ KLADRUBER
From Czech and Slovak regions of Europe. First bred in 16th century, for Emperor Maximilian II. Often used on farms and in dressage competitions. Black or grey. 16-17hh.

HARNESS HORSES

⬇ NONIUS
Hungarian. Named after an Anglo-Norman stallion that founded the breed. Black, bay or brown. Has a large size range – from 14.2-17hh.

➡ WIELKOPOLSKI
Polish. Many types: heavy ones are used on farms; light ones to drive or ride. Usually bay, brown or chestnut. About 16hh.

DRAUGHT HORSES

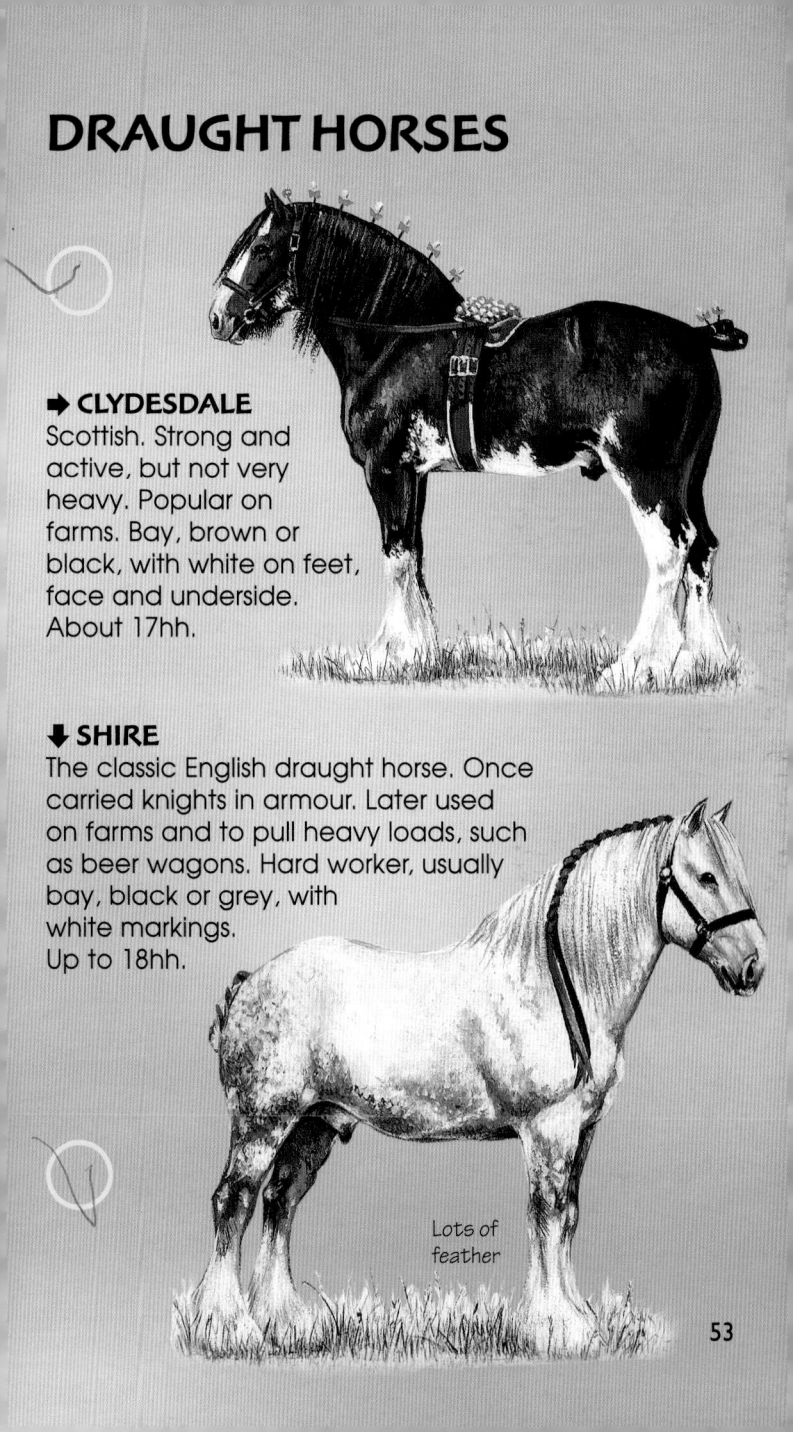

➡ CLYDESDALE
Scottish. Strong and active, but not very heavy. Popular on farms. Bay, brown or black, with white on feet, face and underside. About 17hh.

⬇ SHIRE
The classic English draught horse. Once carried knights in armour. Later used on farms and to pull heavy loads, such as beer wagons. Hard worker, usually bay, black or grey, with white markings. Up to 18hh.

DRAUGHT HORSES

➡ SUFFOLK PUNCH
From Suffolk, England. Short and stocky. Does well on little or poor food. Very good-natured. Always chestnut. About 16-16.2hh.

⬅ IRISH DRAUGHT
Good all-round farm horse, from Ireland. Makes a very good sports horse when crossed with a Thoroughbred. Bay, grey, chestnut or brown. 15.2-17hh.

➡ PERCHERON
From northern France. A popular working horse. Very strong. Often weighs over a ton, but needs little food. Good to work with. Black or grey. 15.2-17hh.

⬅ ARDENNES
From France and Belgium. Was used by Napoleon's cavalry. Powerful but gentle. Can live out in bad weather. Chestnut, roan or bay. About 15.2-16hh.

For a link to a website with lots of horse sound clips, turn to page 60.

DRAUGHT HORSES

↓ BRETON HEAVY DRAUGHT
From northwest France. A strong, rugged working horse. Usually strawberry roan in colour, but can be bay or chestnut. 15-16hh.

→ PINZGAUER NORIKER
The oldest Austrian breed. Quiet and strong. Excellent for pulling ploughs. Bay, chestnut or spotted. 15-16hh.

➡ AUXOIS
Ancient French breed. Once used for carriage and farm work. A powerful working horse. Usually bay or strawberry roan. Never black or grey. About 15.2hh.

⬅ TRAIT DU NORD
From northern France. Similar in shape and temperament to the Ardennes. Quiet and gentle. Usually bay, roan or chestnut. About 16hh.

DRAUGHT HORSES

➡ AVELIGNESE
Bred mainly in Tuscany, northern Italy. Originally used as a pack pony or a light draught horse. Short and muscular. Usually chestnut. About 14.2hh.

⬅ VLADIMIR
From Vladimir, Russia. Used for heavy and light harness work. Bay, roan or chestnut. About 16hh.

➡ JUTLAND
Danish. Once used by the Vikings. Used mostly as a farm horse and as a brewers' draught horse. Chestnut, black, grey, bay or light brown. 15.2-15.3hh.

➡ SCHLESWIG
From northern Germany. Once used to carry knights in armour. Now used mostly on farms, and for haulage. Nearly always chestnut. 15.2-16hh.

⬅ DUTCH DRAUGHT
An ancient, pure breed. Traditionally used on Dutch farms. Very placid. Strong and hard working. Grey, bay or chestnut. Up to 16.3hh.

➡ BOULONNAIS
Bred in France for the Crusades. Later used as a farm horse. Strong and good looking. Grey, bay or black. About 16.2hh.

INTERNET LINKS

If you have access to the Internet, you can visit these websites to find out more about horses and ponies. For links to these sites, go to the Usborne Quicklinks Website at **www.usborne-quicklinks.com** and enter the keywords "spotters horses".

Internet safety

When using the Internet, please follow the **Internet safety guidelines** shown on the Usborne Quicklinks Website.

WEBSITE 1 Lots of horsey activities, puzzles and tips on how to look after a horse.

WEBSITE 2 An interactive guide to looking after a pony.

WEBSITE 3 Try a puzzle about legendary horses, then click on their images to read their stories.

WEBSITE 4 Watch a video clip and discover fun facts about Przewalski horses.

WEBSITE 5 Test yourself on the parts of a horse's body.

WEBSITE 6 Watch video clips of horses, play horse games and take a tour of a horse farm.

WEBSITE 7 Lots of horse sounds to listen to.

WEBSITE 8 Simple animations of the different ways horses move.

WEBSITE 9 Video clips of Lipizzaners performing amazing dance movements.

WEBSITE 10 Horse puzzles and quizzes.

WEBSITE 11 Online exhibits from a horse museum.

Usborne Publishing is not responsible and does not accept liability for the availability or content of any website other than its own, or for any exposure to harmful, offensive or inaccurate material which may appear on the Web.

USEFUL WORDS

all-rounder – horse or pony that is good at different things, such as hunting and gymkhana games.
cob – short, stocky horse (about 15.3hh). Quiet and well behaved.
colt – male horse up to three years old.
dressage – training of a horse to master basic skills plus more difficult, precision movements.
event horse – used in horse trials, which include dressage, show jumping and cross-country riding.
filly – female horse up to three years old.
flat racing – racing over short course without jumps.
foal – horse or pony up to one year old.
gelding – male horse that has been operated on so that it cannot breed.
gymkhana – show where short races and mounted games are held.
horse – fully grown horse that is over 14.2hh.
hunter – strong horse that can gallop cross-country and jump fences.
hurdler – horse that races and jumps small barriers, called hurdles, usually over courses about 4km (2½ miles) long.
mare – female horse over three years old.
pony – fully grown horse that is under 14.2hh.
school master – old, well-behaved, well-schooled horse or pony. Safe and reliable for people learning to ride.
show jumping – jumping competitions.
show horse/pony – competes at horse shows in one, or several, classes of competition. Judged on its appearance and schooling as well as suitability for the class entered.
stallion – male horse (not a gelding) more than three years old. Can be very difficult to control.
steeplechase – race run over fences on courses about 7km (4 miles) long. Name comes from old English tradition of racing between church steeples.

SPOTTER'S CHART

The horses and ponies on this chart are arranged in alphabetical order. When you see one, write down the date in the blank space next to each name. You might like to jot down the name of the place where you saw it, too, for a more complete record of your spotting.

Name of breed	Date	Name of breed	Date
Akhal-Teke		Connemara	
American Saddlebred		Criollo	
Andalusian		Dale	
Anglo-Arab		Dartmoor	
Appaloosa		Døle	
Arab (any type)		Don	
Ardennes		Dutch Draught	
Auxois		Exmoor	
Avelignese		Falabella	
Barb		Fell	
Boulonnais		Finnish	
Breton Heavy Draught		Fjord	
Budyonny		Frederiksborg	
Camargue		Friesian	
Caspian		Gelderlander	
Cleveland Bay		Gotland	
Clydesdale		Groningen	

Name of breed	Date	Name of breed	Date
Hackney		Pinto	
Haflinger		Pinzgauer Noriker	
Hanoverian		Pony of the Americas	
Highland		Przewalski	
Holstein		Quarter Horse	
Huçul		Sable Island Pony	
Icelandic		Schleswig	
Irish Draught		Selle Francais	
Jutland		Shetland	
Karabair		Shire	
Kazakh		Standardbred	
Kladruber		Suffolk Punch	
Knabstrup		Tarpan	
Kustanair		Tennessee Walking Horse	
Lipizzaner		Thoroughbred	
Lusitano		Trait du Nord	
Morgan		Trakehner	
New Forest		Turkoman	
Nonius		Vladimir	
Oldenburger		Waler	
Orlov Trotter		Welsh Cob	
Palomino		Welsh Mountain	
Paso Fino		Wielkopolski	
Percheron			

INDEX

Akhal-Teke, 39
American Saddlebred, 33
Andalusian, 37, 44
Anglo-Arab, 32, 42
Appaloosa, 33
Arabs, 6, 7, 8, 32, 36, 37, 40
Ardennes, 55
Auxois, 57
Avelignese, 58
Barb, 37, 45
Boulonnais, 59
Breton Heavy Draught, 56
Budyonny, 38
Camargue, 29
Caspian, 28
Cleveland Bay, 49
Clydesdale, 53
Connemara, 23
Criollo, 28
Dale, 21
Dartmoor, 22
Døle, 42
Don, 38
Draught horses, 4, 7, 8, 53-59
Dutch Draught, 59
Exercising, 13
Exmoor, 6, 22
Falabella, 29
Feeding, 13, 14-15
Fell, 21
Finnish, 50
Fjord, 26
Frederiksborg, 51
Friesian, 47
Gelderlander, 47
Gotland, 25
Groningen, 48
Grooming, 16
Gudbrandsaal, see Døle
Hackney, 49
Haflinger, 25
Hanoverian, 43
Harness horses, 4, 7, 46-52
Highland, 20
Holstein, 43
Hooves, 17
Huçul, 27
Icelandic, 26
Irish Draught, 54
Jutland, 58
Karabair, 39
Kazakh, 27
Kladruber, 51
Knabstrup, 44
Kustanair, 50
Lipizzaner, 44
Lusitano, 37
Markings, 9
Measuring height, 11
Morgan, 34
New Forest, 23
Nonius, 52
Oldenburger, 48
Orlov Trotter, 46
Palomino, 40
Paso Fino, 35
Percheron, 55
Pinto, 40
Pinzgauer Noriker, 56
Points of the horse, 10, 11
Polish Arab, 36
Ponies, 20-31
Pony of the Americas, 31
Przewalski, 6, 30
Quarter Horse, 35
Riding horses, 32-45
Riding styles, 18
Russ, see Gotland
Sable Island Pony, 31
Schleswig, 59
Selle Français, 42
Shagya Arab, 36
Shetland, 20
Shire, 53
Shoeing, 17
Stabling, 13
Standardbred, 46
Suffolk Punch, 54
Tack (saddles and bridles), 19
Tarpan, 30
Tennessee Walking Horse, 34
Thoroughbred, 7, 8, 32
Trait du Nord, 57
Trakehner, 41
Turkoman, 41
Vladimir, 58
Waler, 45
Welsh Cob, 24
Welsh Mountain, 24
Wielkopolski, 52